BONSAI

by Kenji Murata
&
Keiji Murata

translated by
Tsutomu Kanô

edited by
Don Kenny

HOIKUSHA

Contents

(Cover Photo)
    Japanese White Pine — Formal Upright

BONSAI

by Kenji Murata & Keiji Murata
translated by Tsutomu Kanō
edited by Don Kenny

 No. 29 of Hoikusha's Color Books Series. Published by Hoikusha Publishing Co., Ltd., 17-13, 1-chome, Uemachi, Higashi-ku, Osaka, 540 Japan. ISBN 4-586-54029-X. First Edition in 1974. Tenth Edition in 1983. Printed in JAPAN

Japanese White Pine — Formal Upright

Here is an excellent example of the formal upright style. Japanese white pine stands strong and erect, its roots gripping the earth evenly around the base and the trunk tapering off at the top. The balance is maintained by the harmonious placement of the branches. It bespeaks the grandeur of a towering, magnificent tree.

Japanese White Pine — Twin Trunk "Dusk"

Creative Trees for Bonsai

Not every kind of tree is suitable for Bonsai. It must be able to live in the confines of a pot and respond to cultivation and training so that the most beautiful natural aspects of the tree may emerge according to a preconceived design. Most important, it must adapt naturally to dwarfing techniques and should therefore, not grow too rapidly or profusely. The leaves must be small and detailed, getting even smaller with proper trimming. Dwarf trees produce the best small leaves. The tree must be strong, and able to withstand strenuous training without trouble.

Japanese White Pine – Twin Trunk

    This tree stands in suspended motion, almost like a painting.

Japanese White Pine – Three-Trunk Style

These three "trees" are all growing from the same root. The height, thickness and curves have been grown to achieve matchless harmony. This tree is said to have had close to one hundred years as a Bonsai.

Japanese White Pine – Rock-Grown Style (below right)

This style, also known as "clinging-to-a-rock," is achieved by planting the roots in peat muck that is smeared over parts of the rock. This one appears as an old pine growing in clusters on the rocky top of a mountain, or as an isolated boulder or island, tufted with pine.

Japanese White Pine – Rock-Grown Style

What stands out in this Bonsai is the masculine quality that can be felt in the gripping tenacity of the roots on the rock. It looks strong and permanent. The pot seems slightly too small in comparison with the tree, however.

Japanese White Pine

Japanese White Pine — Root Connected
(Reminiscent of a coastal scene)

Over half the trees used in Bonsai are evergreens, and of those, fifty percent are Japanese white pines. The species is strong and is an integral part of Japanese scenery. Its needles are short and grow densely and it can be trained easily into various forms, making it a relatively "safe" tree for Bonsai. It grows slowly and will maintain the same shape for many years. It takes a long time for the bark to appear old, however.

Japanese White Pine — Root Connected

If fertilizer and water are given too frequently the needles will grow too long and too rapidly, requiring careful trimming and modification. Unlike other pines, the buds do not grow and they are not pinched, as a general rule. A young tree of this kind should be repotted every two or three years, and an old tree, every four or five years in the spring, when the needles are slightly hard. It should be given a lot of sunlight and the needles should be sprayed regularly in the summer.

Japanese White Pine

Japanese White Pine – Root Connected

Although the trunks all appear to be independent trees, they share the same root. This formation can be found in nature also. And sometimes a tree blown over by wind or rain will send its branches up as trunks, becoming the root itself. This tree makes one almost hear the sound of waves as one looks on a scene that perfectly evokes a pine grove by the sea.

Japanese White Pine – Twin Tunk (left)

Also called "growing up together," this is a tree with two trunks grown from the same rootstock. Careful planning will create a pleasing balance of heights, thicknesses and positions. The tree here has good proportions and the branches are well placed. Its only defect is that the main trunk hardly tapers at all from the middle part to the top, and looks a bit like a pillar.

9

Japanese White Pine – Twin Trunk
(Still a young and straightforward tree)

Japanese white pines can be trained into many shapes, but since the needles tend not to be uniform, they are generally not planted in clusters. As in the photograph below, however, a variety of interesting forms can be achieved by proper cultivation.

Japanese White Pine – Rock-Grown Style
    Suspended over the top of a waterfall, the branches seem to hang down over a huge rock.

Japanese Black Pine – Formal Upright

Japanese black pine is second only to Japanese white pine in its popularity for use in Bonsai. It has become one of the most typical varieties because of its hardiness and good response to cultivation, and its pleasing green hue that is retained throughout the four seasons. The masculine quality of this species comes out in this tree in the firm roots, the old-looking branches and trunk and the way the leaves grow upward, making an almost perfect Bonsai.

Juniper – Coiled or Sinuous

This tree can grow where the soil is poor, on mountains and rocks, asserting its existence in prolific growth. Since the tree is characterized by very small openings for water absorbtion in the roots, here the trunk has partially died. The curve of the trunk and the bleached skeleton in the middle are typical of the juniper.

Japanese Black Pine — Coiled or Sinuous

A noble tree, with the best qualities of the black pine — scaly bark that is weatherbeaten and rough, and strong, erect needles.

The black pine is well-suited for Bonsai. It is extremely hardy and can survive cold and rough weather, it will not weaken with pruning, and is generally one of those with the most fortitude.

Since it is one of the dryer trees, it can stand in sunlight and usually needs less water than average. It should be replanted once every three or four years during the early part of March, and the needles are trimmed in May or June.

Japanese Black Pine — Formal Upright

This tree is filled with a sense of force, and the bark is truly a work of art.

Related to the black pine, this kind has a peculiarly heavy bark, reminiscent of brocade (*nishiki*), which develops cleavages and splits. It was also called "rough bark pine," or "rock pine." It was very popular before the war. It needs slightly more sunlight than the black pine.

Juniper — Coiled or Sinuous

The special pattern of the juniper turns and twists the trunk and it looks as though nature has sculpted its own design into the wood. It is highly stylized but looks as though it were a unified part of a total pattern that includes the pot. As is always true, a masterly tree needs a masterly pot. This particular pot is about three hundred years old, a rectangular glazed dish made in China and imported about four hundred years ago.

Juniper — Curved or Sinuous

This flowing pattern and the dead wood give the tree a flavor of rich elegance. The pot may appear to be small, but it gives the tree a springboard, from which it seems to bound upward. This is an especially graceful juniper.

Juniper — Coiled or Sinuous

This once grew way at the top of a mountain ravine, with the clouds close by. After transplanting, it remained healthy and can endure all kinds of weather, and has a solemn, patient feeling. Since so much of the trunk is dead, it requires very little water. The dead wood is considered a very beautiful part of the design.

This kind of tree needs slightly more water than the Japanese white pine, and likes water sprayed onto its needles in small amounts. The buds are pinched occasionally in spring and autumn and it should be transplanted every two years between March and the beginning of May.

Juniper — Curved or Sinuous

Saghalien Spruce – Clump

As its name implies, this type of tree is native to Hokkaidô
and the northern islands, and it is a well-loved Bonsai tree. The
five trunks all grow from the same rootstock, and interestingly,
there are no lower branches so that the clusters of leaves
appear to shade the trunks like an umbrella. This is slightly
unorthodox, giving the Bonsai a sense of freshness and
originality.

Saghalien Spruce – Group Planting

This multiple planting includes thirty separate trunks that make a distinctive design from the skillful way they have been arranged. It looks very natural, like a windy wood. In this type it is important to use a species whose leaves will be uniform and regular, otherwise the design will be distorted with new growths of leaves or needles.

Saghalien Spruce – Semi-Cascade

The lower branches are well balanced and firmly in place.

This kind of tree comes from the northern islands of Japan, where the climate is something like tundra with peat bogs washed by frequent rain and dense fog, blessed only rarely with bright sunlight. The Saghalien spruce, acclimated to such conditions, will maintain small branches and short needles, with appropriate care. As a dwarf tree that does not grow quickly, it can bear the harshest weather conditions.

Saghalien Spruce – Triple Trunk

It looks courageous, and at the same time its shape has an almost eccentric sort of grandeur.

This tree has been lovingly cultivated by a certain group of artists since the late nineteenth century, but it was not fully recognized for its potential until around the time of the First World War, when many trees from the north were being brought into the main island of Japan. It appears that the first attempts produced only thousands of dead trees when they were potted, but the masters of Bonsai have found ways to keep the tree strong and responsive to training. Today it is very widely grown as Bonsai.

Saghalien Spruce – Group Planting

Compared with the trees shown on p. 21, this Bonsai has the effect of a deep, primeval forest somewhere far away from the abode of man. The design centers around the balance between two groups of trees, each of which has a main tree central to it. A skillful touch has been added in the way the back trees are smaller, giving a feeling of depth and dimension.

Saghalien Spruce – Twin Trunk

Bonsai as an art was strongly influenced by literati paintings (in the style of the Southern school of China) at its inception, and one can see its effect in these trees. They are neat-looking, almost prim, but also softly elegant. There is nothing profuse here, and no "extra" elements to distract. This style is enhanced by the fine moss placed on the earth, giving the whole a completely natural, and calm feeling.

Saghalien Spruce – Group Planting

One of the assets of the Saghalien spruce is its hardiness – it can withstand cold and damp and pinching the buds does not weaken it. It is easy to cultivate. This "flower of the evergreens" can be enjoyed throughout the year, and since its bark scratches easily, it can be made to look old in a short time.

The needles are sensitive to hot sunlight, so they should be protected from the bright sun in the summer and sprinkled in the evening. The tree takes more water than other evergreens. The shape can usually be controlled by the single process of pinching the buds. It should be repotted every two years.

Saghalien Spruce – Group Planting

An interesting contrast with the previous plate, this Bonsai is in the same group planting style but gives an entirely different feeling of a spot off in the northern tundra.

Cryptomeria – Clump

Using a species well-loved by Japanese, the artist has skillfully brought forth five trunks from the rootstock and created a variation nicknamed "standing soldiers," from the special vigor and erectness of the stance. He has also given distinct lines for the form as a whole and added to its effectiveness through the use of an unusually wide area of ground underneath.

Cryptomeria – Formal Upright (right)

This is the sort of tree one might expect to find within the grounds of a Shinto shrine, and it actually does have some feeling of reverence about it. The spread of the roots and the power of their grip should be noted, and the way the lowest first branch has been shortened. Other details are the highly effective "old" look of the bark and the small dead branches at the bottom that have turned white.

Cryptomeria

Cryptomeria — Formal Upright

Cryptomeria

The cryptomeria has been loved since the early days of Bonsai, for its strength and the ease with which its special qualities can be developed. It grows in majesty among the mountains and mist, here recalling visions of an old tree, somber and respectful, or a lone tree standing in the heights of a mountain meadow. Indeed, solidity and strength, sobriety and calm are best expressed by the cryptomeria.

Since it is a temperate zone tree, it should have abundant sunlight and water, and it likes rather a lot of fertilizer. The buds are pinched in spring and autumn, and a young tree should be repotted every two years, an old tree every three or four years. The tree is also vulnerable to insects and will weaken if they are not controlled.

Cryptomeria — Twin Trunk

Needle Juniper – Twin Trunk (right)

The design of these trees is unorthodox, made more interesting by the feeling of destruction in the large areas of bare wood. As a whole, the secondary trunk is slightly too large, but in this case it adds a somewhat exotic feeling. The leaves are few but they leave exposed the interesting fissures and points of the trunks.

Needle Juniper – Clump (below)

This kind of tree appears in the *Manyôshû* (an anthology of poems that was compiled in the eighth century) as *muronoki*, and it is also known as *nezu*. Its short needles and splendid forms make it suit Bonsai well. This tree is well-known among needle junipers. The balance between all the components is good, and it has a pronounced personality. Its particularly appealing points are the naked wood in the central trunk and the curves of the secondary trunks.

Needle Juniper

Needle Juniper — Twin Trunk

Needle Juniper — Slanting

Needle Juniper

A tree with a constitution stronger than many of the other pines in Japan, this one also has very fine needles. Its wood is hard and it is amenable to training in the "driftwood" style, and it needs only a small amount of water. It takes less water than the black pine, and buds are pinched occasionally between spring and fall. It should be transplanted every three or four years into a new pot.

White Cedar – Twin Trunk

The white cedar makes a pretty Bonsai, attractive to anyone, but it does not have much personality of its own. It grows almost anywhere and can be easily found by collecting. It takes strong root but should be protected from extreme cold and heat. It needs slightly more watering than average and buds that have grown long should be pinched twice in the spring and once in autumn. It should be repotted every two years.

Seigen Red Maple — Triple Trunk

    This is a maple for which Japan is known, and is often exhibited. It has been cultivated as Bonsai since the Tokugawa Period (1603–1868). The trunk is simply rounded, in contrast to the rough or faulted examples of pines, and here, the balance of three is pleasing. The roots appear to be entirely natural and familiar. There is no feeling of monotony in the trunks, which are not actually very tapered.

Seigen Red Maple – Slanting

This small tree with its beautiful tiny red leaves looks as though it were coming into new bud. The trunk can become uninterestingly uniform but there is power in the thickness around the joints. It is apparently difficult to achieve good balance between the shape and the healthy, bright colored leaves.

Japanese Maple — Slanting

Japanese Maple

A deciduous tree native to Japan, it is even better known than the red maple, and along with the Tang maple and zelkova, it is one of the most commonly used deciduous Bonsai trees. Its assets are the straight simplicity of the trunk, the softness of the branches and the exquisite delicacy of the leaves. There are many horticultural varieties such as red maples which are less common and highly valued.

For cultivation, pinch the buds from time to time as they grow long and prune the ends of the branches so that they will not absorb too much energy from the rest of the tree. Pruning must be done without delay to keep the branches slender as it is important to keep the lines soft. It should be watered once or twice a day in spring and fall, and in summer two or three times. A young tree should be repotted every year.

Tang Maple – Formal Upright
    This tree has small leaves and an appealing agedness in its bark.

Maidenhair Tree — Formal Upright

This was originally a Chinese tree. It is extremely strong and with each passing year it develops roots that grow to look like icycles winding around the trunk. The female tree produces copious ginkgo nuts and in autumn the leaves turn a cool yellow. This example is truly typical of the natural maidenhair, in the thickness of its trunk and the balance of each part.

Japanese Wax Tree — Informal Upright

The wax tree was originally imported from Okinawa to use as the base of a vegetable dye for textile dyeing. Its red autumn leaves almost match the red-leaved Japanese maple in brilliance. It grows very quickly however, when it is young and is difficult to keep in shape. For that reason it is often trained as above in informal, twin trunk or multiple planting styles. For a wax tree this one has been shaped well and has retained a very natural feeling.

Tang Maple — (rough bark) Formal Upright

This is the Tang maple, and its leaves are divided into three points like a frog's hand. It is a plain, rustic tree, but has more endurance than the Japanese maple, and is stronger. It lives a long time. It is one of the most interesting trees among Bonsai because of the roots, which converge and finally knit together, creating a table-type of cover over the earth. Cultivation is very simple, requiring careful pinching of the buds and shoots, and when two or three shoots appear, one should be continuously snipped, and the leaves pruned in early summer. Otherwise, its care is very like that of Japanese maple.

Climbing Maidenhair Tree

The strength of this tree is unusual, giving new shoots a special vitality and dense growth. There are almost no cases when it is damaged by insects. It is somehow appealing for the other-worldly quality of its appearance and for the yellow leaves in the fall. As a Bonsai, its strength adds to its beauty. It can be monotonous, however, and some find it distasteful. Its cultivation is not difficult. New shoots should be snipped around June. Watering is average, and it should be repotted every year.

Beech – Group Planting

Botanists call this *inu* beech. It grows in mountain meadows, and is a tall, deciduous tree that is easy to cultivate. The young tree is strong, and planted in group style because it has very wide appeal. This illustration is not a very skillful one, but it was created with the intention of appearing "natural."

Beech – Group Planting

This example is a rather skillful attempt at expressing a wood or grove. The artist has used trees all with the same tiny leaves, planted them together and has achieved a sense of fine detail in the design as a whole.

Beech — Rock-Grown

This gives a feeling of a tree growing in the mountains rather than on a plain. The roots of these three old trees grip the earth firmly, and they have begun to adhere in a way to suggest the passing of many years. The trunks tend to be uniform, but the branches have interesting turns and fall softly at the ends.

Beech – Informal Upright

This is the same genus as the tall deciduous trees, the chestnut, oak, and others. They are characterized by the dead leaves that cling to the branches all winter long instead of falling off. It appears simple, and rather desolate in that condition. It is hardy and requires no special methods, as it can tolerate cold weather. The new shoots are pinched off only once a year and trimming the leaves should not be done. It takes slightly more water than average and needs repotting every two years.

Hornbeam – Group Planting

This is part of the birch family. The trunk has especially interesting potential for design and the branches will grow densely. It has fine leaves somewhat like zelkova leaves, but it curves much more graciously than the zelkova. Its care presents no special difficulties except that new lines should not proliferate too much. If possible, the leaves should not be trimmed. It does not require too much water.

Zelkova Tree – Formal Upright

This is one of the most common deciduous trees found in Bonsai. The trunk is round and faultless and the tips of the branches are soft. This is one example of the "broomstick style" which is achieved because of the fineness and density of the branches as they seem to sweep the sky. The lower right-hand branch, like a broom leaning against the trunk, breaks up the main line and makes an interesting new design.

Zelkova Tree – Formal Upright

All unnecessary elements have been removed in planning the distribution of branches in this tree, creating an idealized tree in an appropriate pot. The branches begin about one-third the way up the trunk, then they become rather dense, creating a rhythmic design.

Japanese Maple – Formal Upright

The form here is reminiscent of the maple, with dense twig growth and a sense of detail. This tree is still too young, but with some time the bark can be made to look mellowed and old.

49

Zelkova Tree

The zelkova is one of the most common of all Bonsai trees. It differs with location, type and so forth, but it usually has small red new shoots, giving it the nickname "red sprout." Its small leaves also make it a good Bonsai tree. It seems to have a youthful vigor in the prolific new shoots it constantly sends out. It is strong and the tips of the branches are pliable and firm.

It will not wither, but it grows quickly, and the leaves tend to grow long. The trunk is also vulnerable to damage and the forking of branches tends to sap energy from other parts. Thus, shoots must be trimmed many times over from spring through the end of summer, and particularly vigorous branches should be pruned.

Japanese Wax Tree

The wax tree is the source of the ingredient for lacquer, and also has beautiful leaves in the fall. The red of its leaves is deeper and more brilliant than even the maple, appearing as though it were dyed. It is pleasant to look at when the dark brown fruit is on it, or in the spring with the new buds.

It is strong and likes sunlight, and its cultivation is relatively uncomplicated. It will also live a long time. The young tree puts forth many shoots that will grow if not controlled. It is, therefore, relatively difficult to train, although there is potential in its basic qualities. It should not have too much water and when the new shoots have appeared, they should be trimmed, leaving two of the original leaves and cutting the new ones. That will cause new buds to grow. It should be protected from the hottest part of the summer and the cold of mid-winter by keeping it in temperature-controlled places. Repotting should take place in the spring, just before the new buds open.

Zelkova Tree – Broomstick Style

This is a pretty example of the broomstick style, created by the fine and soft branch tips.

Pink Japanese Apricot

There are well over three hundred kinds of flowering apricots, but for Bonsai the most common are the meadow, pink and scarlet varieties. Unlike the meadow (or wild) apricot, in winter it has much pinker blossoms. Note the beautiful aged quality of the bark and the way the branch extends over the circle of the pot, adding an interesting dimension to the balance.

Japanese Apricot — Curved Style

This is a strong mountain tree whose flowers are white — a first rate Bonsai. The aged quality of the trunk gives it a certain elegance, and truly impressive contours have been achieved in the curve of the trunk and downward swing of the branches.

Japanese Apricot – Old Tree

The rustic quality comes out strongly here in the thrust of the branches. The "old" flavor has been especially well preserved.

54

Flowering Japanese Apricot

This tree is one of the favorites, for its perkiness even in the cold of winter, for its copious, pert flowers and for the soft perfume that they bring. It has been loved by many, many generations of Japanese.

Wild Apricot Group

This was originally a strong mountain meadow tree with early-blooming and copious blossoms. They are usually red, pale red or pink. Rare examples have eight-petaled blossoms. Both the trunk and branches have their own interesting idiosyncracies. Both are small, as are the leaves, but with flowers the tree becomes noble. Most apricot Bonsai are this type of tree with its sweet-smelling blossoms.

Naniwa Apricot Group

Blossoms come late, and they are round in shape, mostly with eight petals. Most are white, or uncommonly, light red. This tree has especially strong-perfumed flowers. The leaves are also a circular shape. This tree is also common in Bonsai.

Red Brush Group

Like the tip of a brush, the ends of the buds have a bright red coloring that adds gaiety to the whole tree.

Bungo Apricot Group

These have either large double or single flowers, but both are impressive, refined trees. They do not, however, give off perfume.

Other types of Japanese apricot (or plum, as it is commonly called), include the *kôbai, hibai, anzu* and *makô* groups.

Crimson Japanese Apricot — Informal Rock-Grown

This resembles the scarlet apricot except that the color of the blossoms is deep crimson at the edges. There are not many of this kind, and for Bonsai, they are very difficult and thus, extremely rare. This example is famous for its bark appearing old and weathered and its form settled. What is interesting is the rock, which looks like a swaying ship. The unusual structure of this Bonsai produces a highly sophisticated harmony between the reddish rock and the red of the flowers, carrying one into a fantasy world of esthetic pleasure. See the close-up on the next page.

Japanese Apricot — Old Tree

Japanese Apricot

Apricot trees need a lot of sunlight and much water should be given when the earth below looks white with dryness. It is also helpful to spray the buds when they begin to form. After the blossoms have fallen and the new buds begin, old branches should be clipped, and after the new shoots have grown somewhat, they should be pruned. Since the second budding will not produce flowers, one must be very careful to leave enough flowers on. Fertilizer is applied in May or June, and August or September, five or six times, using oil cake, bone meal, potash or some other kind. Repotting takes place every year, middle to late March.

Crimson Japanese Apricot — Old Tree

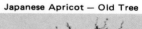

Japanese Apricot — Old Tree

Winter Jasmine — Informal Upright (Slanting)

Winter jasmine is also called "Spring flower" blooming in the early spring, and it is well-loved for Bonsai although it is quite different from the red-flowered apricot trees. It is strong, but grows too quickly to be easily trained as a Bonsai. This example is an unusually successful one, with firm roots, dense twigs at the ends of the branches, and appearing to be very natural.

Flowering Quince — Red Flowered Strain

    This tree has red and white blossoms, but the red type is especially beautiful. It is a dwarf tree, and produces abundant round and small flowers that come out almost steadily throughout the four seasons. It is very difficult to train as a Bonsai, but such wild, natural effects as the one below can be achieved.

Flowering Quince — Informal Upright

There are many varieties of this tree, but they all grow fairly densely. The trunk is thin and bent, and the slender branches tend to grow upward at a slant. Blossoms come before the leaves in late March or early April in an eye-opening red. There is fruit, but it turns yellow on ripening. The color changes in the fall. This particular variety shown is unique and its blossoms can be enjoyed almost all the year around. One must not forget to water it, and give it sun and slight breeze when choosing a location. It cannot attain the desired effect of a thick trunk, but unnecessary shoots should be pruned in order to preserve the shape.

Winter Flowering Quince – Root Connected

Another of the quince family, this one is accustomed to slightly colder temperatures. It gives an extraordinary plethora of blossoms. It blossoms a bit too late, however, to be a true "winter" flowering quince. Blossoms can be red, mostly single petal, or white, or red and white mixed. The leaves are small, and the branches grow in wave-like patterns. It is a good tree for cultivation as a Bonsai. Give it plenty of water, sunlight and breeze, and be careful not to let it get too cold in winter. Buds should be pinched at appropriate places when they come out.

Cherry Tree – Informal Upright

The cherry is Japan's national flower, but there are actually very few Bonsai grown from this tree. There are not many naturally dwarfed types, and the leaves are prone to grow too large. This tree is still young, but the form is pleasing.

Korean Cherry Tree

This is a tree that came from South Korea in the late twenties as a Bonsai. Even growing old, it did not grow very large. It has weathered bark and nicely bent branches, and the abundance of flowers makes it a good Bonsai tree. This old and elegant tree is a very fine and unusual Bonsai. The small, circular flowers are neat, like dancing butterflies.

The Flowering Quince Family

They can be roughly divided into the hardy winter flowering type, and the spring flowering type. The former one blossoms early and has medium large circular flowers with a fresh, bright color. The trunk, however, is not thick, and the branches are thin and dense, and the leaves are small. The later-blooming spring type has a good thick trunk and rather larger leaves. The blossoms are a deep color. The examples of below and above right have the white pots which enhance the tree well. Below right needs a few more branches.

Winter Flowering Quince — Sinuous

Winter Flowering Quince — Clump Style

Winter Flowering Quince — Clump Style

Tôyô Nishiki Flowering Quince

This is a horticultural variety that is also a member of the flowering quince family. It is healthy and easy to cultivate. It is unique because its blossoms may combine red, white, and cream in one tree. The blossoms are thick and round, and single-layer. In April when they bloom, the tree is luxuriantly beautiful.

Tôyô Nishiki Flowering Quince

The thick trunk, and the upward direction of the trunk and branches make this an interesting Bonsai tree. It is deciduous, and has strong new shoots. It is hard to train and retain the shape, but it does have a wild, natural appearance. It will live a long time. This example is an excellent achievement for Bonsai in the decisive, yet mature feeling of the trunk and branches and it retains the essential quality of the species.

Japanese Dwarf Cherry — Old Tree

Cherry Tree

There are many kinds of cherry tree, but the best loved one for Bonsai is the Fuji cherry. Its name derives from the fact that it grows abundantly around Mount Fuji. This one, taken from its natural environment and dwarfed, has a strong frame and its flowers are elegant light red circles.

Other than the Fuji, cherry is not often used for Bonsai, but the Korean cherry is occasionally seen and is highly prized for its tiny round flowers and its response to cultivation as a

Japanese Dwarf Cherry — Young Tree

dwarf. The winter cherry usually makes a good dwarf tree with pert, thrusting branches and an abundance of bright red flowers from the early spring. It makes a treasured Bonsai.

Cherry trees need slightly less water than average, and the leaves on the Fuji cherry should be protected from the heat of midsummer sun and from the cold of mid-winter, using a screen or placing it in another spot. The branches should not become too long and dense, and care should be taken to prevent harm by insects.

Crab Apple – Slanting

An old saying uses this tree in a metaphor for a beautiful woman with a lovely form. In the spring some of the more mature buds should be pinched from the ends of the small branches, and the blossoming that follows offers a magnificent sight of countless pale red flowers. It is a deciduous tree native to China and the way it stands makes it easy to train as a Bonsai. It is one of the oldest cultivated flowering trees. This tree seen here is old, for a crab apple, and a famous Bonsai.

Crab Apple – Slanting

Bonsai of this crab apple (*Malus Halliana*) have been a well-known specialty of the Nagoya region for a long time. It is very frequently trained into the "octopus style" with clusters of branches becoming the "legs." This illustration shows how amenably it curves and how it is bent about a third of the way up the trunk. This example is fresh and vigorous as it is still young.

Juneberry — Semi-Cascade

A thick, heavy trunk suggests the long life and durability of this tree.

The flowers come out in April or May together with the leaves, and they have five layer medium sized petals. If one looks down on the tree in bloom, it gives a feeling of soft, fleecy down. There are small berries that come after the flowers and ripen into a dark color in the fall, remaining for a considerably long time. The naked tree with no leaves is stark, but somehow refined.

The tree has good limbs and injuries heal quickly, making cultivation easy. It needs ample water and just as the buds appear, they should be sprayed. Pruning takes place after flowering but since new shoots are few, this pruning should be light.

Azalea

This is a tree native to Japan. It is strong, grows very quickly, and will respond to training into any shape. The flowers come out in many colors and different configurations, depending on the kind of azalea. There are almost countless different kinds. It needs ample sunlight and water and new buds should be pinched early, leaving two or three leaves. When still growing, the flowers are a pale color. A young tree should be repotted every year, and an old tree, every two years, after the blossoms have fallen. It should be planted in light clay soil mixed with sand and some sphagnum moss, to which a little black loam is added.

The Garden of a Bonsai Cultivator

The garden of a Bonsai cultivator is a riot of color in the months of March and April. Lined up on the benches, these flowering Bonsai burst out one after another in beautiful color. Pictured are flowering quince, crab apple, apple, pear and others, all blossoming in profusion. They are placed to face south, giving them ideal exposure to sun and wind. Most flowering Bonsai cannot tolerate cold temperatures, so in the winter they should be placed under cover but left open to the south in a way that air can freely penetrate, and the earth should be covered with a protective material. The number and density of blossoms varies with each type of tree, but fertilizer that will penetrate the cilia of the roots will be effective in causing the tree to blossom well.

A Room Brightened by the
Presence of a Flowering Bonsai

Holly — Group Planting

The roots seem to grow together completely naturally.

The special feature of this tree is in its small and juicy red berries that darken when they fall off. This deciduous tree will grow almost anywhere. It is strong, with small leaves, and makes very good Bonsai. It is important that it should be watered regularly, and it needs sun and good ventilation, and slightly more than average amounts of fertilizer. Unnecessary new shoots should be removed early and new buds should be pinched off in late spring.

Fruited
Maidenhair
Tree

Maidenhair Tree

This tree forms a family, genus and species by itself, but there are many variations in maidenhair, nonetheless. Those used for Bonsai are the fruit bearing type, and the climbing maidenhair.

Fruited Maidenhair Tree

The name of this type in Bonsai refers to the female that produces copious berries. One can distinguish between male and female trees by whether or not their leaves are cleft.

Climbing Maidenhair Tree

The name of this tree refers to the many roots it produces that begin to grow upward around the base, appearing to "climb."

Magnolia – Twin Trunk

The flowers are six-petal, and white, and they give off a sweet fragrance. In March, before the leaves come out, one blossom appears on the end of each branch. This kind of magnolia is very valuable for its flowers, but there are almost no suitable ways to train it into a Bonsai. The formal upright style is probably the best, but as one can see in the plate, the style appears to be rather tentative.

Camellia – Horticultural Mountain Camellia

    This is a strong tree whose bark and lines appear to gain force and character with the years. It has big, medium green leaves that make it a pleasant tree to look at with flowers or without.

Gardenia — Clump

Idesia — Slanting

Little Crab Apple — Slanting

This is a dwarf apple tree whose fruit comes heavily and abundantly, leaving the leaves to pop out here and there in bunches. It needs much more water than average, and flourishes if bone meal is added to the fertilizer. It should be transplanted every year in about April.

Spike Winterhazel — Formal Upright

This tree belongs to the family of *Hamamelidaceae.* The
leaves should be trimmed in the spring and about seven or eight
flowers will appear in the same place. It has a unique beauty
about it, but the branches tend to grow long very rapidly and
the trunk takes a long time to thicken. Thus, there are almost
no good Bonsai of this tree. It has, like others, its own peculiar
shape to begin with.

Little Crab Apple – Slanting

This is a horticultural dwarfed tree that is one of the smallest of the apples and has very small leaves. It is used quite a bit for Bonsai. Trim it in April or May, and flowers will follow. Since the buds are red, sometimes when the white flowers come out there is a trace of red left in them. In July or August it puts forth tiny little apples. There are not many of these that have been trained into good Bonsai, but the one below, cultivated for a long time, is certainly an exception.

**Fleshy Fingered Citron
— Semi-Cascade**

Other Bonsai Fruit Trees

There are many other fruit trees besides those we have discussed that become good Bonsai, including the chestnut, Korean bush cherry, oleaster, and many others. One of the interesting ones is the horned orange whose name in Japanese is derived from the appearance of many protruberances from the end of the orange, like a Buddhist monk's two hands placed together in prayer.

Persimmon — Slanting

Chinese Flowering Quince — Formal Upright

Red Sandalwood — Small Bonsai

We have touched on the main types of Bonsai trees, including the evergreens, deciduous trees, flowering trees, and others, but we have not talked about the various grasses, herbs and shrubs that can add so much to the sobriety and interest of a fruit tree Bonsai, for example. There are other trees such as the pear, peach and so forth which have both pretty flowers and interesting fruit, and those such as the persimmon and the English holly whose fruit is the center of interest. We do not judge a Bonsai fruit tree on the basis of the size, gaudiness or number of fruit but rather on the general flavor of the season, the natural appearance it gives the tree and the sense of place that the fruit offers the viewer.

Little Loquat — Small Bonsai

Dwarf Japanese Sweetflag

Trees Conducive to Training as Small Bonsai

The qualities most important for Bonsai are small leaves, dense and thin branches, first of all. Second, one desires strong and full blossoms that will be followed by healthy fruit.

Little Crab Apple
— Small Bonsai

Persimmon — Small Bonsai

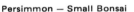

Little Loquat – Small Bonsai
This is an admirable little Bonsai.

Needle Juniper — Small Bonsai

This has good thick leaves and well-formed trunks.

Needle Juniper — Formal Upright

Even as a small Bonsai, this tree has an air of nobility. There are very few that have been trained to this point.

Japanese Black Pine – Small Bonsai

This has the extravagance of literati-style Bonsai. It harmonizes well with the rock placed nearby.

Bonsai are often distinguished by size, which is measured from the base of the trunk to the tip. Large ones are usually over 90 cm, medium are about 50 cm and small ones are up to 10 cm. Recently there has been a kind of Bonsai boom among modern Japanese who enjoy brightening their apartments with these little trees, and the small size is the most popular right now. Whereas large and medium Bonsai take about 10 to 30 years to mature into their full shape, faster-growing trees of small size require only 3 to 4 years; an evergreen trained for 7 to 8 years ought to be quite respectable.

Cultivating Small Bonsai

One can grow and train a small Bonsai starting from seed, collecting, or from a new shoot made from a cutting. Starting from seed, there will be some results in two or three years. Unlike large Bonsai, the small size can be achieved by anyone, with little difficulty, and it takes a relatively short time. Perhaps it is for that reason that these are called "Bonsai for the people."

Small Bonsai can be made by using pincers or scissors, and while one works one has the joy of almost watching it take shape. For example, when a branch appears on a formal upright style, you should cut off the trunk directly above it, and when, the following year, another branch develops on the other side, the trunk cutting is repeated. The result is a tree shaped like a backwards "Z." Without wiring or other techniques, almost all deciduous trees can be treated this way.

Display of Small Bonsai

It should be repotted in about April — for deciduous trees, once every one or two years, and for evergreens, every three of four years. Cease adding fertilizer one and one-half months after repotting, and after that sprinkle on a little thin fertilizer two or three times a month. In the winter place the tree under a slatted frame open at the south.

Some trees usable for small Bonsai include trident and Japanese maples, and Kaidô crab apple.

The difficult part is watering. Since the pot is so small, if the water runs out it can cause much harm, especially in the spring when the plant dries out quickly. It should be watered three times a day, morning, noon and night. On a very windy summer day, it can take as many as six waterings. For those who really love their plants this will be no trouble, but others, less patient, will need the assistance of family members. At any rate, it is worth a try to see if one can create a treasured little tree at home.

Pots for Small Bonsai

These are all from a kiln in Kyoto, but they include pots of all different kinds, shapes and colors. Just looking at them is enjoyable. It is possible to get relatively good pots today at very reasonable prices.

The Spirit of Bonsai and Techniques of Cultivation

The Spirit of Bonsai — Its Essense and Variety

What is Bonsai?

Bonsai is the art of growing sturdy and simple trees in pots and caring for them so that they will reveal the innermost beauty of the natural plant in the process of cultivation. Bonsai can be decorative, blossoming forth at certain times of year, or they may form unusual patterns with their leaves, but more than those qualities, they represent the distillation of the best and most beautiful attributes given to them by nature.

Such trees have been variously described as "scale reductions of nature," or "imitation nature," or "reproduced natural artlessness in trees," but none of these fully describes the heart of Bonsai. They emit more than a sensation of nature in miniature. To try and truly understand is to embark upon a long and rewarding journey of the senses that is difficult to describe in a few words. One could, for example, carefully dig up a small tree and begin cultivating it at home, but no matter how meticulously one worked, or for how long, the simple process of creating a miniature tree will fail to capture the natural environment and aura of that tree, even if it is reduced perfectly hundreds of times smaller. Many, however, will be unable to discern the difference between a scale model and a Bonsai, admiring the precision of the miniature and believing it to be superior artistry. For them, it is a cute toy, like a model train or car in which the detail has been well preserved.

There is no tree in nature, young or old, that is quite the same as another. Each is unique, depending on the land, climate and surrounding environment. And every tree is molded by its species and the special characteristics of its family, giving it a personality of its own and a unique appeal. At the heart of Bonsai is careful choice, to look at many and select one whose form is good and whose appearance leaves one feeling somehow impressed. The beauty that is in and around the tree must be incised into the memory, for it is that memory which will become a tool in creating the form and feeling in the Bonsai.

This statement, by a committed devotee of Bonsai, is to me one of the deepest expressions of appreciation that I have ever heard. It sums up the instinctual feeling of Bonsai that, if one can develop the same, will open the way to understanding their special quality.

Strictly speaking, then, Bonsai are not miniature copies of natural trees, but they are artificially perfect or ideal trees created to grow in a pot that enhances their beauty. Their creation is based on the emotional response to a tree "whose form is good and whose appearance leaves one feeling somehow impressed." It may be that such an ideal tree cannot be found anywhere in nature. Bonsai are, indeed, more natural than nature itself.

Pondering the origins of Bonsai, it is easy to imagine our ancestors, born into the beautiful and varied land of Japan, awed and moved by the rich scenery around them. The emotional impact of nature perhaps compelled them to search in nature for an ideal. It was from this feeling and the yearning to create, with nature as both the subject and medium, that the art of Bonsai was born. Bonsai — a natural scene that moves the feelings and senses made to live in a tree created as it stands in a vessel — this most perfect form of the natural tree is almost inexpressibly profound.

Many Kinds of Bonsai

Bonsai include a huge variety of trees that differ in species, shapes, sizes and details, making them endlessly interesting, and widely appealing to people everywhere. They may be classified in three general categories — type of tree, style, and size.

A. Types of Trees

(1) Evergreens

These trees retain their green leaves, regardless of season. They are used for decoration, display, or special occasions in which they are often the central ornament. The most common are Japanese black pine, Japanese white pine, Saghalien spruce, cryptomeria, needle juniper, and juniper.

(2) Deciduous Trees

Bonsai cultivators generally call trees that are not evergreens deciduous. They include the following rough categories:

a) Red autumnal leaved trees. These are valued for the green of their leaves between budding and early summer, and for the beautiful red and yellow of their leaves in the fall. They have their own special kind of naked beauty in the starkness of the winter. They include Japanese maple, zelkova tree, Chinese nettle-tree, beech, wax tree, oak, and maidenhair.

b) Flowering trees. These beautiful and elegant trees are prized especially for their flowers, and they include Japanese apricot, flowering quince, winter jasmine, crab apple, cherry, peach, magnolia, camellia, and azalea.

c) Fruit trees. The chief kinds are persimmon, pear, chestnut, Chinese flowering quince, holly, idesia, little crab apple, fleshy fingered citron and red sandalwood.

Some people plant herbs and shrubs in their Bonsai but these are added to enhance and supplement the tree, and cannot properly be called Bonsai themselves. Likewise, orchids or such plants as *Rhodea japonicum* are not exactly the same thing as Bonsai.

B. Styles

(1) Formal Upright

The trunk in this style of Bonsai is maintained straight and erect, a single trunk stretching upward to the sky. In that perfect form the roots are firmly implanted, reaching out in all four directions from the trunk, giving a feeling of stability. The trunk has a feeling of power, gradually tapering off in thickness as it rises. The branches reach out from either side in almost perfect symmetry. This kind of Bonsai makes one think, for example, of a lofty, grand old cryptomeria standing proudly in a meadow, towering upward.

(2) Slanting

Here, a single trunk leans slightly to the left or the right. If the formal upright can be taken to symbolize "constancy," then the slanting might be the symbol of "change." This style usually involves growing the roots all on one side, and the branches also, to become a form that one can imagine leaning over the edge of a high, windy cliff, or on the side of a deep ravine.

(3) Coiled

This style is also made with a single trunk, but rather than growing straight, it winds and twists in either direction, moving forward and backward as well. It evokes wild, windswept storms tearing around the tree and giving it a force and splendor that is hard to emulate. The roots are usually very thick, and the bark is coarse. The branches are also twisted into the pattern of the tree.

(4) Semi-Cascade

This is grown from a single tree whose trunk leans slightly and whose branches lean just a bit over the line of the edge of the pot. Those Bonsai whose branches hang considerably over the edge of the pot are called cascade style, but for reasons of display, that kind is not very popular today. Both cascade styles remind one of a tree perched at the edge of a very steep precipice, constantly moved by a strong wind.

(5) Twin Trunk

This is a tree which was grown to develop two strong trunks when it was a young plant, a main trunk and a secondary trunk. Harmonized in height and thickness, they make a combination that produces a beautiful synthesis. This is also called "growing up together" by some. The so-called twin tree style also involves two trunks, but in that case the Bonsai is actually two separate trees with their own roots.

(6) Multiple Trunk

Here, a single plant is trained so that several, or even dozens, of separate trunks grow out of the same plant. The number of trunks can range anywhere from three to thirteen, or even higher, but they are customarily an odd number. This is an interesting shape for one plant to take, but the final effect is that of a small forest or grove. The style used to be nicknamed "standing soldiers."

(7) Root Connected

The prototype for this kind of tree can be found deep in a mountain forest where sunlight only rarely filters through the thick growth, and where a fallen tree will take root in a very special way. It produces a long and tortuously winding single root from which many small trees develop, although the appearance is that of several separate trees.

(8) Raft

This might be called a man-made type. The trunk is placed on its side and the branches are then made to grow upward, the trunk then becoming the root. By inarching grafting the roots can be made to grow in the desired position. The natural sinuous type is, of course, the more valuable.

(9) Multiple Tree

This type of Bonsai consists of nine or more trees, mostly or all of the same species, planted together in one container and arranged in a carefully worked-out design to appear as a forest, a wood, or a row of trees. Species may be combined, such as zelkova with Japanese white pine, but aftercare and training are much more effective and easy if they are of the same family. Balance and coordination of forms is also much less frustrating if the species are not mixed.

(10) Clinging to a Rock

One must have a large rock with an appropriately big depression in it to plant several trees whose roots will ultimately wind themselves around the rock in the desired way. The Bonsai becomes a scene evocative of a mountain-top or a lonely island in the middle of the sea. It is often placed in a large, flat container that has water in it to increase the island effect.

These are the basic styles of Bonsai. Others include the informal upright – a single trunk with balanced and wholesome curves that grow softer toward the top – and the exposed root style, in which the roots are purposely trained to remain partially above the ground, often rising relatively high.

C. Sizes

The size of a Bonsai is usually judged by the height of the tree. There is no fixed standard of measurement, but the proper height can be determined from the size of the room in which the tree will be displayed, and the height that can be most fully appreciated in the surroundings. It should not go much above ninety centimeters, and perhaps the standard size is about forty-five centimeters. Bonsai can be large (ninety centimeters or more), medium (about forty-five centimeters), or small (ten centimeters or under). There is again no fixed standard, but a tree about the height of a cigarette (seven to eight centimeters) is usually considered small, while those under that size would be "miniature" Bonsai.

STYLES OF BONSAI

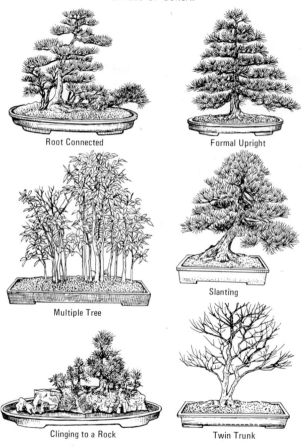

Root Connected

Formal Upright

Multiple Tree

Slanting

Clinging to a Rock

Twin Trunk

Techniques of Cultivation — Methods and Skills

What is a Good Bonsai?

Before going into the techniques of cultivation, we must ponder for a moment exactly what a good Bonsai is. There are several important elements in judging which points of the tree should be emphasized and developed in order to create the most beautiful and expressive possible tree. One can put any amount of devoted work into cultivating a tree but if he does not know what to aim for, if he is not clearly aware of the concrete qualities that will make it a true work of art, then his efforts will be meaningless. A fault, for example, must be treated with great care, especially by the beginner. There are many instances where a fault may be a glaring contradiction to the "rules" and actually enhances the tree to the extent that the Bonsai will be a superior achievement. Somewhere, outside the prescribed forms, that fault becomes the source of an esthetic quality that in some delicate way affects the whole appearance of the tree.

This does not mean that a fault can always be made into an asset. A master, it is said, can experiment with the most sensitive points of his work, but those who have just begun would do better to follow established forms. It would profit him more and result in more honest work if he leaves the purposeful certain use of faults to the mature artistry of the masters.

A good Bonsai, then, remains to be defined. It is, of course, a tree that incorporates the several elements considered necessary for a beautiful tree. The trunk, branches and all the other elements of the tree must be beautiful in their own right. But even more important, the Bonsai will be judged on the basis of the harmony between the pot and the overall effect of the tree. I would like to discuss here the elements in the tree itself that will help in creating a good Bonsai.

(1) Spread of the Roots

The roots and the way they spread are of utmost importance in the overall appearance of a Bonsai. There is no feeling whatsoever in a tree that looks like a telephone pole poked into the ground. The roots should be exposed, rising above the ground, and they should surround the tree in a way that harmonizes with the style. They lend a feeling of powerful exertion as they grip the earth under the trunk.

Bonsai connoisseurs have a special name for regular roots that extend out in four or eight directions, and this pattern is considered very classic and valuable. The roots of maples, if left for many years, will develop abnormally and will begin to coalesce, eventually forming a solid mass of root that looks like a table. This can produce a very interesting effect, but there are other possibilities than the four-direction or table-type patterns. The most important factor is that the roots be strong, giving the impression that the tree is imbedded permanently in the earth. The beauty of the roots lies in that sense of stability as they grip the firm, well-packed earth around the tree. Thus, in the cascade style, for example, the roots will naturally form on one side, adding to the natural dynamics of the position of the tree.

(2) Trunk

The trunk is the central feature of the tree. "Trunk, one; branches, two; roots, three" is an old expression of this priority.

It is the central element in the form of a Bonsai, like the skeleton of a man.

The trunk should stand easily and firmly, gradually tapering towards the top. The best trunks are round, gentle ones, not harsh like an upturned chopstick. Something just sticking into the ground straight up is indeed dull. A Bonsai trunk needs some pattern in it, some feeling of nature in the large, no matter what its size. The bark is best when it appears to be old — an effect that can be produced by the popular technique of roughening the bark. The core has an important function as the central locus of the life of the tree. It becomes the symbol of the tree as a whole. Thus, if the core is broken, or if its location is not clearly defined, the tree will not be suitable for Bonsai. The core should be the vibrant center of a vigorous tree, giving strength and continuity to the entire length and line, and becoming the source of elegance.

Some very interesting Bonsai are actually constructed on the bleached-out skeleton of the core. These are usually cultivated from old mountain trees. They have the dignity of pain, as though they had bravely battled the elements over long years and survived, the scars remaining. Other peculiar trunk types are the distorted "twisted trunk," bumpy "wart trunk," the old-looking "rough trunk," and the interesting "brocade trunk." These are prized for their idiosyncracies, and definitely constitute an exception to the general rule that a "good" tree has a firm, naturally rounded trunk with no conspicuous aberrations.

(3) Branches

The branches in a tree are like the pattern in a textile;

without them, there is no design. In general, a young tree has upright branches, while those of an old tree tend to droop downward. It is not necessarily pleasing, or good for the tree, to allow too many branches on a Bonsai. The most interesting trees are planned around a design in which the branches hide the trunk in some places and reveal it in others. It is important to control the distribution, thickness and length, as well as the direction of growth of the branches, changing them if one is too fat, too long, or if its direction destroys the balance. It is necessary to remove unwanted twigs or sprouts, and to discipline one that is growing at a destructively fast rate. We have mentioned some of the general standards by which to judge an offensive branch, and it is easy to understand why a branch that grows across the front of the trunk must be removed or trained so that it will not spoil the line. Branches that grow close together or radiate out from the same or proximous joints are unsightly and heavy, while two branches that extend left and right at about the same level look too much like a bar across the tree. These, too, must be radically modified, usually by cutting. A drooping branch is another possibly distracting element but in many cases this tendency can be utilized to add interest to the tree.

The lower part of the branch must always be free of leaves or twigs so that the spread of the roots and the line of the lower trunk may be properly seen. It is standard practise to have one branch extending from a spot one-third the distance from the base to the top of the trunk as the lowest branch.

(4) Leaves

Some craftsmen of Bonsai believe that a tree does not need leaves to become a work of art, but considering the character of

Bonsai — a work of art created in a living plant — and the design appeal in the leaves, it would seem barren without them.

In any case, the leaves should look strong and vital, filled with color. As they shed their light on the tree they add a whole new dimension to its appearance. Because Bonsai are made to be small, they need the tiny, delicate presence of leaves to harmonize with the small trunk and branches. Without them, the tree becomes simply a deformity of nature. There are, nonetheless, certain kinds of trees that no amount of cultivation or training will reduce, and so it is necessary to choose one that has fairly small leaves to begin with. The leaves of dwarf species and eight-segmented species are especially well-liked for Bonsai. The leaves need not be always thick and dense. In fact, if they are growing too thickly the result will be a tree whose design is spoiled by blatant blocks of solid leaves. The effect of branches peeking out from gaps here and there among the leaves, and showing some expanses of branch is far more appealing.

(5) Flowers

Since evergreens so often make truly magnificent Bonsai, we cannot say that flowers are a necessary element, but still, a flowering Bonsai is one of the most beautiful. A few, graceful and refined flowers will be more dignified than copious blossoms all over the tree, and harmonious distribution, as well as proportionate size, are naturally assets. The number of flowers differs with each kind of tree. Clusters of blossoms on a crab apple or a flowering quince, for example, are truly impressive, whereas one or two white plum flowers can be called nothing but exquisite.

(6) Fruit

Many of the same principles for flowers also apply to fruit. The important point to remember is the balance between the fruit and the tree as a whole. A lot of fruit is not necessary, but a harmonious balance with the tree is. A good Bonsai will produce with its fruit an echo of the universal bearing tree, its activity and season radiating from the natural balance of the tree. Further, since the tree is often seen during the display season of fall and winter, the pleasure will be greater if the fruit is a bright and cheerful color in contrast with the bare branches.

Finally, in addition to these important elements in judging whether it is a good one, or not, perhaps the best practical way to understand is to see as many living examples of the art as possible. A practised and critical eye is one of the most valuable skills there is in creating Bonsai oneself.

Methods of Cultivation

There are two main methods. One is to find or buy a tree that has already been trained to some extent and then continue to train it as one desires. That is, in effect, a remaking of a tree already begun. Of course the value of the tree will rise, even double after a while through the efforts invested in it. Unlike other arts such as painting or sculpture, Bonsai is literally alive and growing. It can change and its value changes with it.

The other method is to begin cultivation with a seedling. This is a method that requires many years but it is reliable and if one chooses to train one of the more suitable species, it more often yields better results than the remodeling method. To remake a tree that has already been trained to some extent is not something that just anyone can do, and for that reason our discussion here will focus on the second, more general method of cultivation from seedlings.

There are in actual use today about seven methods of obtaining a seedling for cultivation – collecting, layering and dividing, dividing roots, using cuttings, grafting, growing from seed, and using a shoot. We cannot describe them all in detail here, but will concentrate on the easier ones at which even an amateur can succeed.

(1) Collecting

This method involves the cultivation of a young, perhaps naturally dwarfed tree that was selected from among many trees growing in a meadow for its suitability for Bonsai. If one walks in the woods in a somewhat high or hilly region he will find young beeches or clusters of flowering quinces, and if one looks closely, very few have trunks that are not bent or branches that are not overdeveloped. But to find one from among them to dig up and cultivate oneself is deeply satisfying.

The sapling tree should be healthy, straightforward and with the smallest possible leaves. The trunk should be straight and strong, and it is desirable to find one with some interest in the design of trunk and branches. The proper timing varies a bit with the species and the environment, but March or April is about right for a warm climate and May or June if the climate is much colder than temperate. The tree should be dug up before the new roots have developed too much and new buds have opened. To uproot it when they have become strong and active could do irreparable harm to the tree.

Next, when uprooting the wild seedling, it is essential not to pull, but to dig it out very carefully avoiding damage to the bark and cutting as few roots as possible, especially the taproot. The tree will usually not take root again if the earth is removed from around the cilia. When a suitable tree has been found, prune away the weeds surrounding it and dig in a wide circle around it with the base of the tree in the center. Use a small trowel or shovel and be careful to retain as much earth as possible. Dig deeply down and under, cutting the very long roots as low as you can, using scissors for the taproot if it is too long. Cut off the small unnecessary branches or ends of overextended branches. Water the earth clod with a pipette and cover the roots with straw or wet sphagnum moss, wrapping them around with newspaper and firmly tying them.

When the seedling has arrived at your home, remove string and cotton and shake very lightly. The extra soil will fall away. Look carefully to find roots that protrude from the earth. These should be trimmed with a sharp knife. It is best to plant it in a deep unglazed training pot that has been properly prepared. Over a layer of rather coarse gravel on the bottom, the main soil, which is a medium loam, is added to fill the pot about three-quarters full. Set the seedling in the pot on the bed of loam and gently work it in, covering the top with more loam. Using a chopstick, work the soil in between the roots until no more holes appear, and the soil has penetrated evenly (sand can be added). Jab down the top of the main soil.

Then, spray with a fine watering pot, giving it ample water, until it begins to flow out through the hole in the bottom. The tree should be placed under a screen out of the wind for about twenty days, protected from direct sunlight. Some sun should reach the base of the trunk only. It must be kept watered, but the earth should not be spongy, neither should the top soil ever dry out completely.

The species differ, but for most sprouts will appear in twenty to thirty days. The appearance of new shoots and the leaves opening are certain signs that it has taken root. At that point remove the screen and start giving it direct sunlight a little bit more each day. A tiny bit of fertilizer may also be added. There are many exceptions, but since long shoots may spoil the design of the tree, they should be trimmed, leaving no more than the necessary number of branches. When the new shoots are about three centimeters long, pinch off at the joint, and in about two weeks, two or three more shoots will appear at the same place. Do not let them grow. Only the necessary branches should be allowed to grow. If the tree is weak, however, and you wish to thicken the trunk, leave the new shoots without cutting.

To protect the tree from dryness and coldness in the fall and winter, leave it in a sunny place where the water drainage is good, and cover it with a layer of warmer earth and cotton or sphagnum moss. Don't forget to water it. In the spring the pot must be changed and training will begin.

(2) Cuttings

Strong wild saplings collected from the woods put out new shoots very frequently, but most of them should be removed to use them for cuttings. Therefore, inserting them into soil where they will take root, not only prevents wasting the shoots but also provides an easy way to grow a tree from an old tree, using the stem or branch. It is a very widely-used method. There are actually about five different kinds of cuttings — leaf, new shoot, stem, branch and root. Here we will discuss a cutting taken from a new shoot. It should be taken and placed in soil in the early spring from mid-March to the end of the month, when the new buds begin to swell. A young, new cutting is much stronger than an old one. Cut the shoot at a slant with a sharp, small knife just below the node, and remove one-third of the bottom and top leaves to reduce the water-evaporating surfaces. Keep it moist, place it in a bucket of water until planting.

Use clean soil that will retain water and make certain there is good drainage. Red loam mixed with sand in 7/3 proportions is suitable, and a pot or wooden box may be used. It should not be too deep. Line the bottom with gravel for draining and add clay or fine loam to a level well below the rim, gently pressing down the surface. Plant obliquely, pressing in gently, about one-third of the length of the cutting, into a partially prepared hole. If there are many, do not plant them too close together, and make certain that they will not fall over. Spray with plenty of water. Until new roots appear, do not expose it to direct sunlight, and shelter it from the wind. It helps to water the leaves also, but not too frequently as growth of the roots will be delayed. Water should be given two or three times daily. After one month new shoots will appear. Increase the sunlight each day, and add a little fertilizer. Keep it out of the wind in winter, in a warm place, and water regularly.

(3) Growing from Seed

This method is enjoyable but takes a long time, depending on the species, from planting the seed to a mature tree. If it is to be a small Bonsai, it may take two or three years. The best kinds of trees for this method are Japanese black pine, Japanese white pine, cryptomeria, maple, wax tree, and zelkova tree. The time for sowing is early spring, between middle and late March. Sprinkle powdery soil in an unglazed shallow pot and add a mixture of clean black or red loam with a little sand, and make sure that the pot has good drainage. The seed (if many, they should not touch) is placed on the top of the soil, and then a layer of topsoil is added. Give it plenty of water and keep it out of the wind, in the shade for half the day. It should never get dry, but it should also not be exposed to long or hard rain. Some species will produce shoots in one or two months, while others will take until the following spring. When germination occurs and shoots appear, place it in the sunlight and give it ample water. When two or three leaves have appeared, small amounts of fertilizer may be added. Avoid western exposure in the summer and protect from frost in the winter.

(4) Seedling

In a way it is safer to buy a seedling or naturally stunted young tree that has been cultivated for one or two years since uprooting, from a trusted dealer or nursery. Repotting a young strong tree is the method with the least risk involved. Buy one that is as small as possible, with firm roots, a straight trunk and well placed branches. The season is not fixed, unless one plans to train it immediately, in which case it should be obtained and potted between March and May, or September and October. Those that have been kept with their roots wrapped up should be potted during the last two weeks of March. If it is wrapped, plant it as soon as possible in an unglazed pot. It is of course safer to buy one that has been in the earth rather than wrapped up.

The Elements of Training

In the cultivation of naturally stunted young trees, wild saplings, seeds or cuttings, training can be carried out gradually when the root is firmly developed and strong. Proper training will create a tree, whatever the species, whose inherent beauty and characteristics will be brought out to perfection. For this one must have creativity and certain techniques at hand. In a natural tree, which is unused and its potential untapped, one can find a hidden splendor in the undeveloped beauty of the basic lines, bringing the tree from its natural level to a level of perfection in Bonsai. This process is called "training," but it actually involves a great many steps. They may be roughly grouped into trimming, pruning and wiring. Training techniques vary according to the species, and they also include pinching back the buds, suspending branches, using a jack to correct defects, and others. Here we will take up those methods that are necessary for all species and that may be easily learned by the beginner — trimming and pruning. Trimming is the removal of buds by pinching off, and pruning is the cutting of the branches and roots.

(1) Pinching Buds

Trimming is done because much of the energy of the tree is concentrated in buds and new shoots. In order not to destroy the balance and to maintain a level of energy in other parts of the tree, especially in those branches that must grow stronger, trimming is carried out. It also helps to shorten the line of certain branches and it will accelerate the forking of small twigs, causing the leaves to grow smaller. Thus, trimming comprises an important step in bringing out the full beauty of a Bonsai, in creating small branches and leaves. It is an essential part of training. Methods differ according to species. however.

The Japanese black pine should be trimmed only once a year, when the new buds are fully developed, between mid-June and mid-July. The bud is pinched off with pincers. Care should be taken not to remove any of the old needles which grow just behind the bud, and to leave a few new needles. The timing will vary slightly according to the temperature of the area. About one month after removing new buds, more will appear in the same place, but these will cease to grow before full development, and the length of the needles will be in good proportion to the size of the Bonsai.

Trimming is not generally done to the Japanese white pine. It usually does not put out second shoots if the first are removed, or if it does, they are not uniform and can spoil the design of the tree. However, once a year the new needles on this kind of tree should be pinched off only on those branches that are not growing uniformly and only if they are strong. This serves to preserve the balance of the tree. The needle juniper, cryptomeria and Saghalien spruce, among others, require frequent trimming as they put out new buds prolifically. In general, a few of the new needles should be left, pinching out the others with the fingers. The cryptomeria is especially sensitive to metal.

Species such as the juniper and white cedar put out pronged buds which should be twisted off every time they appear. Care is needed with the juniper and others whose needles can easily be pinched too far down. When this happens, the needles of the cryptomeria will fall off, or if the tree is not at its peak of strength parts of it may wither. The deciduous leaved trees such as maples and zelkova must be treated with precision and gentleness in trimming and since the small branches must be allowed to grow thickly, one has to watch that they are constantly trimmed and not permitted to grow too long. Trimming must be done all through the season between the development of buds in spring and the shedding of the leaves in the fall. The buds on flowering trees such as the Japanese apricot, cherry and flowering quince should be left to grow and the new twigs that have gotten too long are cut off after flowering but before midsummer. A considerable number of flowers or fruit should be left.

Perhaps the most basic thing to remember in trimming is that the tree has to be strong. Its condition is weak after replanting or potting, for example, and trimming should wait until later. And considering the final desired form of the tree, naturally those branches that will grow to become more important in the design should not be trimmed, and secondary branches should not be allowed to sap the energy of the tree. It is a matter of judgement and care, and an adapting of trimming to the tree and its individual circumstances.

(2) Pruning the Branches

Pruning has one very important function, which is to relieve the burden on the tree of thickly growing branches. Depending on the lighting and ventilation, it can also cause forking of new twigs. Of course pruning also removes unnecessary twigs and helps to form the Bonsai. When deciding which branches to prune, refer to the section on branches that appeared earlier in our discussion of what a good Bonsai is and how it should appear. One must avoid such obvious mistakes as permitting a branch to grow across the front of the trunk or leaving several branches growing out from the same point. Pruning is usually done at mid-growth and during the dormant period. At mid-growth there is a rapid burgeoning of vigorous secondary branches that cause the entire tree to weaken, and the main branches begin to grow heavily in the mid-trunk area. Both of these must be pruned. When secondary branches are at the joint, strong, new shoots soon reappear nearby, requiring much attention. If a stump is left when pruning, it is then gradually cut down and it is safe to cut the parent branch off from the joint.

Pruning during the dormant period between late fall and early spring is done to remove secondary branch stumps or withered branches, or branches that have grown too long, in order to refine the shape of the whole tree. It is important to use sharpened knives, pincers and scissors, and be careful to cut very smoothly. This will speed the process of healing where the tree has been cut.

(3) Pruning the Roots

Roots are like branches or leaves in that they must be pruned, especially when they are replanted. The tiny cilia and small roots should be cut at the time of planting in order to hasten the process of regeneration. A Bonsai growing in a small pot will produce a thick growth of roots if it is a young plant, and after two or three years the earth will clot with roots, and water will no longer penetrate easily. For the sake of the roots, among other reasons, the tree should be replanted. It should change pots, have new earth, and the small roots should all be pruned. The tree will then have a new start for a new phase of growth. All dead roots should be removed at that time, and the taproot should be properly shortened to fit into the pot. The cut should be made diagonally toward the bottom, bringing the knife smoothly across the root to prevent decay.

(4) Wiring

It would be ideal to train a Bonsai using simply the techniques of pruning and trimming, but especially in the case of evergreens, it is necessary to supplement those if the desired form is to be attained. Copper, being soft and pliable, is the most common metal for wiring. The size depends on the tree, but number twelve to eighteen wire are the most frequently used sizes. It must be first annealed in a low-temperature fire of straw and when wiring a tree whose bark is soft, especially the deciduous trees, it should be wound with paper tape. The season for wiring also depends upon the tree but many can be wired between late October and late February. Black pines should be wired between April and late June.

The tree must be studied to decide the overall desired shape and which branches should be wired, after which any remaining unnecessary branches should be cut. The tree is wired in order of trunk, main branch (lowest branch) and the secondary branches growing out of it, then moving up the tree to wire each main branch and its secondary branches. When it is necessary to bend the trunk, the lower end of the wire is inserted into the earth at the base. When wiring branches, the two ends of the wire are placed on separate branches to prevent slipping, and the wire runs under the branch below, placed there very lightly.

Without exerting too much pressure and using the softest possible wire, it should be prepared and measured beforehand. Before placing the wire, the branch to be bent or twisted should be gently bent with the hand back and forth several times to loosen it, and rather than bending it during wiring, the whole branch should be gently bent in the desired direction after it is completely wired. For three or four days after wiring, place the tree out of direct sunlight in a spot protected from the wind and give the leaves plenty of water. It should then be placed out of doors. Since wiring is a correcting method, as soon as the desired result has been accomplished the wires should be removed, in the case of small branches after two or three months, and large branches after four or five months. If the bark is not damaged by the wire, it may be left on for as much as a year without moving any of the wiring, and one may expect almost perfect success.

(5) Leaf Trimming

Except in very special situations, evergreen needles should not be trimmed. It should be done to trees such as the maples whose leaves will reappear more delicate and smaller after trimming and to the trees which one wants to produce many smaller branches. About a month after transplanting and applying manure, all the leaves should be trimmed to leave a stalk with one-quarter of the leaves still attached, using small scissors. The stalks will fall off naturally and in the same place. About two or three weeks later, buds will grow and new leaves will appear. It is as though the leaves were going through two autumns instead of one when the leaves are trimmed, and the tree will produce the equivalent of two years' growth of leaves in one.

The tree needs fertilizing before the leaves are trimmed to strengthen it against the shock, and after trimming water should be sprayed from above. It should be kept out of direct sunlight and wind until new buds appear. Leaves should not be trimmed if the tree is not in excellent health, and if one branch seems to be weaker, refrain from trimming that branch.

Another technique involves the use of dead wood in a tree in such a way as to make it an integral part of the Bonsai design. The juniper, needle juniper, Saghalien spruce and so forth are among the most amenable to this method. Instead of cutting off a dead branch or part of the trunk, it is left and turned to advantage to be used in a special style. Another technique, in a slightly different realm, is to try and make it appear as though the Bonsai soil were itself a part of nature by covering it over with moss, or by planting grasses, herbs or tiny shrubs around the tree. This is more than simply an esthetic pleasure. It is actually good for the soil, and moss or herbs can also play an important role in the atmosphere and appearance of the entire Bonsai.

Moss used with Bonsai should be fine, with a bright, fresh color. A type that will hold moisture well is preferred. The best kinds are the fine, bright green velvet moss and the darker pine-needle moss. The dense-looking *zeni* moss is not suitable. Moss can be gathered in damp and dark places where it grows naturally. After cutting it out with a knife it will continue to grow if it is watered. It is appried to the top layer of soil with slight pressure, and loose sandy soil is placed around the edges. It should be lightly sprayed with water and left for a week in a spot that is shady for half the day. It needs occasional water, and it will soon begin to grow. It should not cover the entire surface of the Bonsai earth but about two-thirds of it, with the top roots in the center.

Herbs and grasses that grow well in Bonsai include those that have tiny leaves and grow out vertically. The most suitable include golden fern, bamboo grass, wild thyme, moss gentian, dwarf sweetflag and others. These usually pose no difficulty and the most important factor to consider is the harmony, balance and overall appearance of the Bonsai as augmented by herbs and grasses.

HOIKUSHA COLOR BOOKS

ENGLISH EDITIONS

Book Size 4″×6″

COLORED ILLUSTRATIONS FOR NATURALISTS

Text in Japanese, with index in Latin or English.

First Issues (Book Size 6″ × 8″)

1. BUTTERFLIES of JAPAN
2. INSECTS of JAPAN vol.1
3. INSECTS of JAPAN vol.2
4. SHELLS of JAPAN vol.1
5. FISHES of JAPAN vol.1
6. BIRDS of JAPAN
7. MAMMALS of JAPAN
8. SEA SHORE ANIMALS of JAPAN
9. GARDEN FLOWERS vol.1
10. GARDEN FLOWERS vol.2
11. ROSES and ORCHIDS
12. ALPINE FLORA of JAPAN vol.1
13. ROCKS
14. ECONOMIC MINERALS
15. HERBACEOUS PLANTS of JAPAN vol.1
16. HERBACEOUS PLANTS of JAPAN vol.2
17. HERBACEOUS PLANTS of JAPAN vol.3
18. SEAWEEDS of JAPAN
19. TREES and SHRUBS of JAPAN
20. EXOTIC AQUARIUM FISHES vol.1
21. MOTHS of JAPAN vol.1
22. MOTHS of JAPAN vol.2
23. FUNGI of JAPAN vol.1
24. PTERIDOPHYTA of JAPAN
25. SHELLS of JAPAN vol.2
26. FISHES of JAPAN vol.2
27. EXOTIC AQUARIUM FISHES vol.2
28. ALPINE FLORA of JAPAN vol.2
29. FRUITS
30. REPTILES and AMPHIBIANS of JAPAN
31. ECONOMIC MINERALS vol.2
32. FRESHWATER FISHES of JAPAN
33. GARDEN PLANTS of the WORLD vol.1
34. GARDEN PLANTS of the WORLD vol.2
35. GARDEN PLANTS of the WORLD vol.3
36. GARDEN PLANTS of the WORLD vol.4
37. GARDEN PLANTS of the WORLD vol.5
38. THE FRESHWATER PLANKTON of JAPAN
39. MEDICINAL PLANTS of JAPAN

SHELLS
OF
THE
WESTERN
PACIFIC
IN
COLOR

Book Size 7″×10″

⟨vol. I⟩ by Tetsuaki Kira
(304 pages, 72 in color)
⟨vol. II⟩ by Tadashige Habe
(304 pages, 66 in color)

FISHES
OF
JAPAN
IN
COLOR

Book Size 7″×10″

by Toshiji Kamohara
(210 pages, 64 in color)